RAT ATTACK

by Lisa Owings

BELLWETHER MEDIA · MINNEAPOLIS, MN

Are you ready to take it to the extreme?
Torque books thrust you into the action-
packed world of sports, vehicles, mystery,
and adventure. These books may include
dirt, smoke, fire, and dangerous stunts.
WARNING : read at your own risk.

Library of Congress Cataloging-in-Publication Data

Owings, Lisa.
 Rat attack / by Lisa Owings.
    p. cm. -- (Torque: animal attacks)
 Includes bibliographical references and index.
 Summary: "Engaging images illustrate true rat attack stories and accompany survival tips. The
combination of high-interest subject matter and light text is intended for students in grades 3 through 7"
--Provided by publisher.
 ISBN 978-1-60014-790-6 (hardcover : alk. paper)
 1. Rat attacks--Juvenile literature. 2. Rats--Behavior--Juvenile literature. I. Title.
QL737.R666O95 2013
599.35'2153--dc23
                                            2012011225

This edition first published in 2013 by Bellwether Media, Inc.

Printed in the United States of America, North Mankato, MN.

TABLE OF CONTENTS

Dirty, Disgusting, and Deadly

What if a rat scurried into your bed at night? It would probably give you the creeps. Did you know that the rat might try to eat you? Rats have been known to attack people in their sleep. They nibble away at flesh with their sharp front teeth. They often **infect** their **victims** with deadly diseases. Could a rat be waiting for you to fall asleep?

Overrun by Rats

A female rat can have more than 100 babies in a year. Most rat attacks happen in places where rats can easily multiply.

Rat on a Rampage

Anastasia and Alexandra were two infants being treated at a hospital in Russia. Nurses came to feed the sick girls but turned away for a minute. They did not see the furry brown creature climbing into Anastasia's bed.

Clever Climbers

Rats can scurry up walls and race across wires. They can even climb up through pipes and into your toilet!

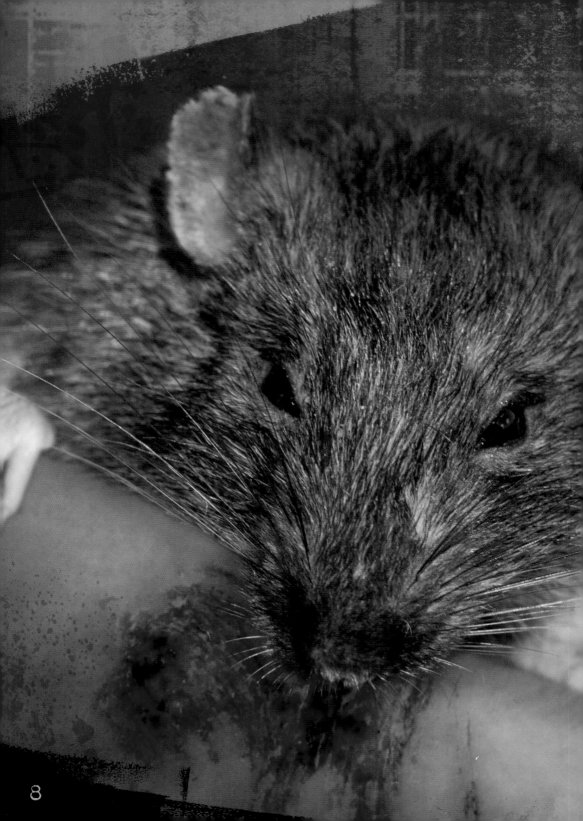

Anastasia was helpless against her filthy attacker. She let out a sharp cry as the rat chewed on her arms. The nurses rushed over and saw the **rodent** jump to the floor. They immediately began treating Anastasia's bleeding wounds. The starving rat was still on the loose.

Nonstop Nibblers

A rat's teeth never stop growing. Rats constantly chew on things to keep their teeth short and sharp.

Alexandra would be the rat's next meal. It scurried over her body. Its long tail trailed behind it. Then the animal's teeth pierced the soft skin of her nose. The rat also nibbled on the tender flesh of her hands. The shocked nurses called for help. The girls were moved to a different hospital to recover.

Bite-Size
Rats are most likely to attack small children. Kids often have bits of food on their faces or hands that attract the hungry rodents.

"We were all scared. The rat was acting so violently."

—Sofia Tulkina, witness

Rescue Gone Wrong

Carol Colburn was relaxing at her home in England. Suddenly she heard screeches coming from her garden. She went outside to see what was going on. A rat was trapped in one of her bird feeders! Carol felt the need to rescue the poor animal. But she did not know the price she would pay.

Carol's husband urged her to wear gloves, but she ignored him. She approached the frantic animal with bare hands. The rat raked its claws over her skin as she struggled to free it. The feeder wire also cut into her hands. Finally Carol gave up. Her son continued with the rescue. Gloves protected him from the **infection** that was already spreading through Carol's body.

Inviting Infection

One small scratch can let in deadly germs. Always wear gloves if you must handle a wild animal. Wash your hands afterward.

Carol was fine for a few days. Then she felt like she had the flu. Two days later, things were much worse. Carol's skin had turned yellow. She could no longer move. The 56-year-old was rushed to the hospital. But it was too late. Carol died hours later of a heart attack. Contact with the diseased rat had proven **fatal**.

Walking Diseases

Rats carry and spread up to 40
dangerous diseases, including . . .

- **Bubonic Plague: This disease killed
  one out of every three people in
  Europe in the 1300s.**

- **Typhus: This disease has fever-like
  symptoms and can sometimes
  result in death.**

- **Leptospirosis: This disease affects
  the blood and organs. Its most
  severe form killed Carol.**

- **Rat-Bite Fever: This nasty infection
  kills one out of every four people
  if left untreated.**

Prevent a Rat Attack

You can prevent a rat attack by making your home ratproof. Seal cracks and fill holes so rats cannot sneak inside. Do not leave food or garbage out. Listen and watch for signs of rats. It is best to contact a professional if rodents become a problem.

Signs You Have a Rat as a Roommate

- Chewing or scratching sounds
- Rat droppings
- Partially eaten fruit or nuts
- Holes, teeth marks, or other signs of chewing
- Greasy smears on wood or walls

Monster Rats

Giant pouched rats can grow to be more than 24 inches (61 centimeters) long. These monsters are believed to have killed at least two children in South Africa.

giant pouched rat

Survive a Rat Attack

If a rat bites or scratches you, make loud noises to scare it away. If it doesn't run off, hit it with anything you find nearby. Clean your wounds immediately. Apply an **antibiotic** if possible. Then visit a doctor. Even a small scratch can cost you your life!

Easy Prey

Rats usually attack people who are helpless or sleeping. This is why babies are often victims. Rats will also attack people who catch them by surprise.

Glossary

antibiotic—a drug that kills bacteria and is used to treat infections and diseases; antibiotic creams are often used on bites and scratches.

fatal—causing death

infect—to introduce bacteria or other germs that cause disease

infection—an illness caused by bacteria or a virus

rodent—a mammal with large, sharp front teeth that are used for chewing

victims—people or animals that are hurt, killed, or made to suffer

To Learn More

AT THE LIBRARY

Eagen, Rachel. *Rats Around Us*. New York, N.Y.: Crabtree Pub. Co., 2011.

Marrin, Albert. *Oh, Rats! The Story of Rats and People*. New York, N.Y.: Dutton Children's Books, 2006.

Person, Stephen. *Bubonic Plague: The Black Death!* New York, N.Y.: Bearport Pub. Co., 2011.

ON THE WEB

Learning more about rats is as easy as 1, 2, 3.

1. Go to www.factsurfer.com.

2. Enter "rats" into the search box.

3. Click the "Surf" button and you will see a list of related Web sites.

With factsurfer.com, finding more information is just a click away.

Index